I0845979

Driving Online Attendance

Social Media and Webinars

Table of Contents

Innovation needs to be part of your culture. Consumers are transforming faster than we are, and if we don't catch up, we're in trouble.

— Ian Schafer

Chapter 1. Introduction

Step into the digital arena with our Special Report: "Driving Online Attendance: Social Media and Webinars". Let us guide you on a lively expedition through the maze of modern digital marketing, underlining the power of social media and the undeniable leverage of webinars - key strategies to supercharge your online audience engagement. In this uplifting, easy-to-absorb report, you'll discover how to fuse traditional webinar wisdom with the unrivaled potency of social media platforms to create irresistible digital experiences for your audience. Embrace the knowledge and let it empower you and your business. By reading this special report, you'll be getting not just an information pack, but a tool set for transformation, tailored to optimise your online platforms. Exciting? Absolutely! So, get ready for a thrilling ride into the future of your digital strategy. This Special Report awaits your curiosity!

Chapter 2. Unlocking the Power of Social Media

In this digital era brimming with possibilities, no measure of success, especially in an online setting, can be exhaustively tackled without delving into the intriguing depths of social media. A master key, albeit a complex one, unlocking the power of social media can open a treasure trove of opportunities that can propel your business towards unprecedented heights.

2.1. Understanding Social Media: The New Marketplace

Social media is not a monolithic entity, it is a sprawling, ever-changing marketplace. It consists of various platforms, from Facebook, Twitter, and Instagram, to niche forums and networks, each housing different demographics and boasting diverse cultural norms and conversation styles. Understanding these platforms individually, noting their intricacies and peculiarities, is the first stride to unlocking their potential.

Facebook, for instance, is incredibly proficient at fostering conversations, offering personal interactions and has a sprawling user base, which empowers businesses to get up close and personal with their customers. Twitter, on the other hand, prizes brevity. It's a fast-paced platform where trending topics wash ashore and recede with startling speed. Instagram is a highly visual platform, favouring striking images and short, impromptu videos. Each platform presents its own, unique opportunities and challenges, and mastering them is pivotal in unlocking the power of social media.

2.2. The Power of Social Media: Where Content Intersects Community

Social media's ultimate power lies in its extraordinary capacity to create and nurture communities around shared interests. It is an online agora where people congregate to share, like, follow, and comment, offering brands a unique vantage point to understand, engage, and cultivate customers. Delving into these specific communities helps businesses tap into the pulse of the market, helping create high-powered, customized content that resonates strongly with the audience.

People, not faceless businesses, craft the language of social media. Understand that language, mirror it in your content, and you will move beyond simply broadcasting to participating. This connection, this dialogue, turns transactions into relationships, fostering trust, loyalty, and high-level consumer engagement. The trick, therefore, is to humanize your brand, put a face to the name, and thread deeper, transformative connections with your audience.

2.3. Building Your Social Media Presence

Creating a formidable social media presence is not an overnight job. It's a meticulous, patient process, built by engaging potential and existing community members, using the right kind of content and tone that suits your brand as well as the particular temperaments of your social platforms. Start by understanding the 'why' of your social media presence. Is it to increase brand visibility? Engage community members? Or solicit customer testimonials and reviews? Having a clear purpose forms a strong foundation for your social media strategies.

Once the 'why' is in place, focus on the 'what'. What are you going to share? Social media is all about sharing content that engages, educates, entertains and excites your audience. Capitalize on the communities you are part of and carefully choose content that will appeal to their sensibilities and align with your brand intent. Make sure to marry this content strategy with the right social media platform.

Ultimately, success in social media is heavily reliant on consistency. Not just in frequency of posting, but also in the tone, nature, and quality of content. Forge a distinct brand voice that aligns with your brand purpose and inject it consistently into your content. Your tone of voice is like your online identity–a distinctive, unifying thread that runs through all your content, offering your audience confidence, familiarity, and ultimately, trust.

Social media platforms can be tricky terrains to tread on, given their ever-changing algorithms and shifting audience preferences. However, when understood and used proficiently, they reveal themselves as truly unprecedented avenues for audience engagement, connectivity, and growth. The power of social media is not merely in its ubiquity but in its potential to unlock unimaginable possibilities. As we've seen, understanding the platforms' unique characteristics, grasping the nature of online communities, and building a consistent, purposeful social media strategy is the key to tap into this power. But remember, this is just the first step. A deeper dive into each platform is necessary to truly wield the power of social media effectively.

Chapter 3. Deciphering Webinar Basics

Webinars, as a tool of digital communication, have enjoyed an increase in popularity within the past decade, largely due to enhanced internet connectivity and the rise of remote work globally. Essentially, a webinar is a seminar that is conducted over the internet, allowing the participants to interact, share, and receive information despite geographical boundaries. Webinars can come in various forms and sizes, ranging from small-scale tutorials to large corporate seminars with a broad, global audience.

3.1. Understanding the Essence of Webinars

Fundamentally, webinars are a unique marriage between education and technology, with the former being the substance and the latter the conduit. As compared to physical seminars, webinars eliminate the confines of geographical limitation, enabling knowledge sharing and interaction on a global scale. A critical aspect of webinars is the engagement between the presenter and audience, usually facilitated through features such as live interaction, chat and Q&A sessions.

Webinars also offer the benefit of convenience. Unlike traditional physical seminars, participants can join from the comfort of their homes or offices, saving both time and travel expenses. Additionally, most webinars offer the facility of recording sessions, thereby allowing those unable to attend at the time of the webinar to view the material afterward – thus extending the reach and lifespan of the content.

3.2. Decoding Types of Webinars

Different types of webinars cater to different kinds of needs. Understanding these types plays a pivotal role in identifying the most suitable format for your intended audience and specific purpose. Some of these types include:

- **Instructional webinars**: These webinars are akin to a virtual classroom. They are designed to instruct or teach the participants about specific topics or skills. Instructional webinars usually involve a span of multiple sessions, almost like a course.

- **Informational or educational webinars**: These aim at sharing knowledge or insights about a particular subject rather than teaching a specific skill or task. These webinars also serve as an excellent platform for thought leaders to share their perspectives and engage with interested parties.

- **Product Demo webinars**: Enterprises often use these kinds of webinars to demonstrate the functionality or benefits of their product or service. They serve the twin purpose of marketing and customer support.

- **Panel discussion webinars**: These webinars usually involve multiple speakers discussing or debating a topic. As multi-view perspectives get aired, these stimulate intrigue and open-minded thought among the audience.

- **Q&A webinars**: This format is typically an engaging and interactive webinar where the presenter or panel elects to answer questions from the audience. It allows both learning and problem solving to occur simultaneously.

3.3. Setting Up Your Webinar

Setting up your webinar is a multi-staged process, comprising both technical and content aspects. Here are some key steps to keep in mind:

- **Platform Selection**: Start by picking a webinar platform. A few factors to consider while choosing the platform includes features, the number of attendees the platform supports, the cost, and the ease of use.

- **Topic Selection**: Choose a topic that will resonate with your desired audience and meet your objectives. A good topic is engaging, relevant, and provides value to the participants.

- **Preparation of Content**: The bulk of your webinar will be defined by its content, including presentations, videos, activities, or even live demos. Design your content to be audience-specific and engaging.

- **Technical Check**: Before you go live, it's crucial to run a test of all technical parameters. Check your audio, video, slides, screen sharing options, etc. Troubleshooting any issues in advance helps ensure a seamless session.

- **Promotion**: Promotion is essential to the success of your webinar. Use your marketing channels, social media, email lists, etc., to get the word out.

- **Follow-up**: After the webinar is over, don't forget to follow up with your attendees. You can send them a thank-you note and share the recording. A post-webinar survey can also help you improve your future webinars.

Having acquainted ourselves with the absolute fundamentals of webinars, we have gained key insights that are to serve as stepping stones for all future endeavors in setting up, running, and succeeding in conducting webinars. This, however, is just the beginning. The following chapters unfold further layers of knowledge needed to not just execute webinars but to amplify their influence and reach in the market. From harnessing the power of content to understanding analytics, from delving into different social media channels to looking ahead at future trends, there is much to cover on our expedition to master the art of webinars.

Chapter 4. Building an Engaging Online Presence

In our digitally infused generation, creating and sustaining an engaging online presence is not just advantageous for businesses, but a necessity. A sound online presence serves as a reliable conduit between the brand and its audience. By standing out in the complex digital juncture, brands can strategically connect and engage with their audiences. With the appropriate guidance, you can steer your brand into the heart of the digital world.

4.1. Forming Your Digital Identity

The first step towards establishing a worthy online presence is creating a significant and relatable digital identity for your brand. This involves understanding your brand's essence: its values, mission, and uniqueness. Remember, this pivotal phase sets the cornerstone for your entire digital marketing journey. This identity should reverberate throughout your website, your social media channels, and across all the content you produce. Building a robust brand identity demands an investment of time and a willingness to introspect and clarify the brand's positioning.

4.2. Curating a Captivating Website

Your website serves as the brand's digital home; consider it the central command of your online presence. Websites need to be engaging, easy-to-use and fully representative of your brand. If you operate within the e-commerce realm, it must offer seamless navigation, secure transactions, and a straightforward buyer's journey. Each webpage should be designed with purpose in mind, offering users not only a visually pleasing experience, but a pathway to understanding your brand, your services and an imminent call-to-action.

4.3. Social Media: Your Digital Billboard

Diving into social media can feel like navigating a labyrinth, but this tool is a potent vector for strengthening your online presence. Each social media platform carries its unique rhythm, language, and audience. Therefore, understanding how to utilize each platform's features and audience preferences is crucial. Always remember, the aim is not just to broadcast your messages, but to engage and grow a loyal community. Manage these digital billboards wisely, and they could effectively steer an audience to your website or webinar.

4.4. Engage Through Consistent Content Creation

Content is king in the digital world. Skillfully crafted content, whether in the form of blog posts, social media graphics, infographics, videos, or webinars, can magnetize your audience. Additionally, regular, consistent, and quality content creation boosts your search engine optimization (SEO), making your brand more discoverable in the online wilderness. A content calendar can help you plan and manage your content creation effectively, ensuring you hit the sweet spot between flooding your audience and keeping them adequately engaged.

4.5. Optimal Utilization of SEO

Search Engine Optimization (SEO) is an excellent tool to refine your online presence and increase visibility. By incorporating keywords related to your product or service, you make it easier for users to find you in their search results. Moreover, creating backlinks to your website through guest blogging or collaborations can significantly bolster your SEO. Remember, SEO is not just about being seen; it also influences the credibility and reliability of your brand.

4.6. Online Interactions: The Art of Engagement

Encourage active participation and engagement from your audience by creating opportunities for interaction. This could be through social media polls, comment sessions or webinars with a Q&A slot. Building and sustaining a participative community online makes your brand feel more relatable and drives audience loyalty. A brand that acknowledges and interacts with its audience fosters trust, a precious commodity in the digital world.

4.7. Learning from Digital Analytics

Lastly, understanding your digital landscape relies heavily on analytics. Make use of the plethora of tools available to monitor and track the metrics that matter to your brand. This can be through in-built tools like Google Analytics for your website or Instagram Insights for your social media performance. Regularly reviewing these analytics provides valuable insights into your audience's behavior and preferences. These data findings grant you the opportunity to refine your strategy and boost your online presence continuously.

Embarking on the journey to establish an engaging online presence can be daunting, but recall, it is quintessential for brands navigating in the digital world. This chapter offers an extensive roadmap that can be tailored to your brand's unique necessities. Fortify your brand's digital voyage with these insightful strategies, and let it be the compass directing your path to success. With persistence, creativity, and insight, your engaging online presence will start to manifest, carving a distinctive space for your brand amidst the digital chaos.

Chapter 5. The Role of Content in Online Success

Unfolding the narrative of online success, wrapped in layers of fine-tuned digital subtleties and strategies, it is impossible to overlook the supreme role that content plays in this dynamic arena. Carefully chosen, meticulously crafted, and efficiently delivered, content is the lifeblood of your digital presence. It is the thread that not only attracts your audience but binds them to you in a web of intrigue, engagement and emotional investment.

5.1. Navigating the Realm of Content

In the vibrant, ever-changing world of digital marketing, the importance of content cannot be overstated. It serves as the foundation upon which your online presence thrives and evolves, blossoming into a robust, engaging platform that captures and captivated your audience. Content is the pillar that supports your online image, chalks out your brand narrative, and determines your relevance in the digital sphere.

It can take a myriad of forms, from blog posts, infographics, and podcasts to webinars, webpages, and social media posts. Each type of content has its unique capabilities and strengths, with their own sweet spots of audience appeal. The trick lies in knowing when and where to utilize them to strike a harmonious blend of diversity and cohesion in your content strategy.

5.2. Crafting Distinct, Quality Content

Quality content has the power to stimulate your audience's curiosity, elicit their responses, and provoke their thoughts in ways that not only enhance their engagement but also foster a sense of connection with your brand. Be it the charm of a beautifully written blog post, the visual appeal of an infographic, or the engaging narrative of a webinar, the essence lies in its uniqueness, relevance, and value.

The challenge is to cultivate your distinct voice in a digital ecosystem teemed with voices, narratives, and conversations. One must devote time and effort into researching and understanding the demographic and psychological profiles of the target audience. Then, the content can be tailored to their interests, concerns, questions, and lifestyle aspects. Remember, content vibrancy comes not just from novelty but from personal resonance.

5.3. Leveraging Social Media to Optimize Content

Social media offers a fertile ground for promoting and optimizing content. With millions of active users, platforms like Facebook, Twitter, LinkedIn, Instagram, and YouTube allow marketers to disseminate quality content and reach out to a larger audience base.

While content forms the backbone, social media acts as a launchpad, an arena where marketers can shape and steer conversations, evoke emotions, and create experiences for the audience. In this process, the content feeds off social media's dynamism and multiculturalism, while the platforms gain depth and substance from the content, forming a mutually nourishing relationship crucial for online success.

5.4. Embracing Content Analytics

Content analytics is the compass that guides your voyage through the digital seascape. It enables you to understand what type of content resonates with your audience, which platforms yield the most engagement, and what tactics work best for your brand.

Google Analytics, Social Media Analytics, and various Content Management Systems offer valuable insights into content performance. Analyzing these data trends can help you tailor your content better, improve audience targeting, and boost your overall online performance. Monitoring how your content performs and adapting based on the findings is as crucial as creating the content itself.

5.5. The Future of Content in the Digital Landscape

The relentless evolution of the digital landscape presents new horizons for content creators and marketers. Virtual Reality, Augmented Reality, and AI are re-defining the boundaries and possibilities for content creation. The potential for immersive, interactive, personalized content experiences is simply astounding.

While the seminal importance of quality, relevancy, and value in content remains unwavering, the mode of delivery is set to witness monumental changes. In this futuristic panorama, the agility to adapt and innovate will determine the success of your content strategy and the prowess of your online presence.

As we navigate the dense maze of digital marketing dynamics, always keep in mind that the spark of your online success rests in the content you produce. It's not just about providing information; it is about telling stories, sparking conversations, and building relationships. It is about turning your audience into your brand advocates.

Chapter 6. Mastering Social Media Channels for Webinar Promotion

A significant portion of mastering social media use in webinar promotion is understanding the nature of different platforms. Let's embark on a deep dive into a handful of notable social media channels, explore those platforms' multifarious features, and discuss strategies for their effective use in promoting your webinars.

6.1. Understanding Social Media Landscape

Foremost, understanding the intricate and diverse landscape of social media is an essential step. Each platform recognized for its unique attributes, user demographics, content format, opportunities, and certain limitations. Therefore, a one-size-fits-all approach can't apply to social media strategies. Instead, it's wise to deliberate the best use of each platform.

6.2. Facebook: The Social Media Juggernaut

Facebook is a dominant force in the social media landscape, possessing a broad range of demographic groups and facilitating various types of content.

For webinar promotion, Facebook can be utilized in several ways. Facebook Events can serve as a public announcement and countdown leading up to your webinar. It provides an opportunity for attendees to engage before the event and facilitates discussions and networking.

Through Facebook Ads, you can target specific demographics that are likely to be interested in your webinar's content. Facebook's advanced profiling and customization features help focus your campaigns directly on your ideal audience, ensuring that your event advertisement gets in front of the eyes of the right users.

6.3. Instagram: A Visual Platform

Instagram's strength lies in its visual-centric approach to content. Imagery and short video content reign supreme here. When promoting webinars, using captivating visuals to trigger attention and interest is the optimal strategy on Instagram.

Instagram Stories, with their ephemeral nature and primary location at the top of the user feed, serve as an excellent tool for reminder-style promotions or last-minute updates related to your webinar.

Moreover, the platform's feature, IGTV, allows for long-form video content that can prove very useful for delivering valuable titbits of your upcoming webinar content, enticing viewers to sign up for the complete experience.

6.4. LinkedIn: The Professional Network

As a professional networking site, LinkedIn is particularly suited to B2B webinar promotion. The platform's options for organic and promoted posts provide ways to reach your professional target audience.

LinkedIn Groups are an underutilized tool that can be exploited for webinar promotion. These groups often form around industry-specific interests, making them prime locations to promote events like webinars that offer valuable insights into the relevant field.

LinkedIn's demographic data can be leveraged to create precise promotional campaigns, directing your webinar advertisement to relevant industries, job titles, or professional skills.

6.5. Twitter: News in Real-Time

Twitter excels in real-time news and quick updates. With its swift interaction and wider organic reach, strategically timed tweets can create buzz around your webinar.

Twitter's hashtag feature should be an essential part of your promotion strategy. Creating a unique hashtag for your webinar not only helps in organizing your promotion content but also encourages conversation and interaction around your event.

Twitter chats - real-time conversations organized around a specific hashtag - can serve as an excellent avenue to discuss your webinar's themes and engage with potential attendees.

To effectively utilizing these and the many other social media platforms, it's crucial to understand what resonates with your audience. Each platform provides unique opportunities for interaction. Your task, as a digital envoy, is to navigate these channels skillfully, delivering the right message at the right time to the right users. Remember, the success cardinal is about creating content that resonates, building relationships, and, ultimately, driving attendance to your webinars.

Let's move from understanding these channels to developing a plan that covers the primary stages of a webinar - pre-event, during the event, and post-event - in the next chapter.

Chapter 7. Increasing Webinar Sign Ups: Effective Strategies

Beginning with a measured understanding of your intentions, outlining a clear and concise strategy for increasing sign-ups to your webinar is a crucial tension point in enhancing audience engagement online. We'll delve deep into the whirlpool of ideas, strategies, and tools at your disposal, unfolding it all in an eloquent but practical approach.

7.1. Understanding Your Target Audience

To talk effectively to your audience, you must first understand who they are. Your target market will dictate the tone of your communication, the platforms you use to reach them and the content of your webinars. It involves a comprehensive examination of your prospective attendee's demographics, psychographics, and behavioural characteristics. By conducting surveys, interviews, or analyzing existing customer data, you can identify key characteristics of your target audience such as their challenges, interests, and wants. All these inform the design and marketing of your webinars, ensuring you offer something that naturally appeals to them.

7.2. Crafting Compelling Webinar Content

The underpinning of a successful webinar is captivating content. Content tailored to answer your audience's questions and solve their problems increases your authority, instills trust, and sparks engagement. Information should not only be beneficial but packaged attractively, using storytelling techniques to elicit emotional responses, thus making the webinars more memorable. Incorporating visual aids can also aid in understanding and retention. However, always ensure your content provides unique insights; generic information can easily be found elsewhere and won't motivate potential attendees to sacrifice their time.

7.3. Creating a Compelling Headline and Description

The first encounter potential attendees have with your webinar is through your headline and description. This initial impression can make or break their decision to sign up. Craft a compelling headline which encapsulates the central theme of your webinar and sparks intrigue. Make it clear, concise, powerful, and if possible, induce urgency. Your description should elaborate on the value proposition of the webinar, detailing what attendees will gain from the session. Incorporating testimonials from past attendees can also imbue trust and validate the webinar's quality.

7.4. Right Timing and Frequency

The timing of your webinar is key in driving sign-ups. You need to understand when your target audience is most active and likely to be available. This could involve consideration of several factors, including their time zones, work schedules, and even cultural nuances. Apart from the timing of the individual webinars, the frequency should also be considered. A well-spaced series can allow for appropriate digestion of information and anticipation for the next, whereas too many webinars may lead to audience fatigue.

7.5. Marketing and Promotion of Webinars

Successful promotion of your webinar necessitates a multi-channel approach. Depending on the profile of your target audience, channels could include social media advertisements, email marketing, blog posts, web banners, affiliated marketing, or even traditional media. Consistency between channels in terms of the message, aesthetic, and timing of communications can provide a seamless experience for potential attendees. The call to action should be clear, enticing potential attendees and making the sign-up process as frictionless as possible.

7.6. Leverage Social Proof

Sharing testimonials from satisfied previous attendees or influential figures in your niche can enhance the appeal of your webinar. This 'social proof' serves to validate the quality and usefulness of your offering, reducing uncertainty for potential sign-ups. Through quotes, video excerpts, or aggregated satisfaction ratings, you can draw upon the positive experiences of others to promote your webinar.

7.7. Utilizing Partnerships and Collaborations

Consider collaborating with industry leaders, influencers, or other brands that share your target audience. This approach can expand your reach, amplify the credibility of your webinar, and provide diversity in content delivery.

7.8. Offering Incentives

People naturally gravitate towards value. Offering incentives such as valuable resources, exclusive content, certificates, or even discounts on your products or services can increase the perceived value of your webinar and consequently, the number of sign-ups.

7.9. Evaluating Performance

After successfully hosting your webinar, evaluate its performance. This involves analyzing registration data, attendee demographics, engagement rates, feedback, and conversions. By doing this, you can identify what worked well and areas for improvement for future webinars, thus instilling a culture of continuous improvement.

Incorporating these strategies in your webinar planning and execution can significantly boost your sign-up rates. Achieving high sign-up rates however is not a once-and-done event but a continuous, iterative process. It involves constantly experimenting with different strategies, learning from previous webinars, and adapting to the changing needs and expectations of your audience.

Remember, the essence of a successful webinar lies not only in its content but also its marketing and promotion - each strategy aligns to the pulse of your audience's needs and preferences. Keep your communication lines open, listen to your audience feedback, and consistently enrich your webinar content and marketing strategies. This way, you build not just an audience, but a community of engaged and loyal webinar attendees.

Chapter 8. Maximizing Attendee Engagement During Webinars

In the contemporary age of digital marketing, webinars serve as an impactful tool in capturing attention and fostering engagement. They offer an interactive platform conducive to learning, discourse, and active involvement, effectively establishing and strengthening connections with your audience. However, successfully maximizing attendee engagement during webinars can be quite the tightrope walk. It involves several elements such as crafting engaging content, encouraging interactions, leveraging technology to amplify engagement, and detailed post-webinar analysis to enhance future experiences.

8.1. Crafting Engaging Content

The foundation of any remarkable webinar is compelling content. Unlike written content where readers have the luxury of skimming through at their pace, webinar attendees need to follow in real-time. Therefore, it is crucial to present gripping and valuable material that keeps your audience interested and engaged. Aim to elucidate your subject matter in a simple and comprehensible manner, ensuring it is informative yet engaging.

For the creation of such content, you should first understand and interpret your audience's needs, problems, and expectations. Market research and user personas play a crucial role here. Once the target audience's characteristics are identified and articulated, you can curate tailored content that resonates with them. Utilize storytelling techniques to connect on a more personal level.

Also, consider segmenting the webinar into manageable chunks instead of one continuous talk. Not only would this lessen the possibility of information overload, but it also provides natural breaks for audience interaction. To elaborate further on this, we'll discuss interactive exercises in our next section.

8.2. Encouraging Interactions

Webinars should not behave as one-sided lectures. Strive to encourage interaction and facilitate lively discussions amongst attendees. Audiences today crave authentic experiences, and interactive webinars can satiate this thirst for engagement. There are many ways to foster meaningful interactivity.

Q&A sessions form the backbone of a dynamic and engaging webinar. They provide the unique opportunity for attendees to engage directly with the presenter, airing out diverse perspectives or seeking clarifications. Periodic Q&A segments throughout your presentation can make it more conversational and guarantee that attendees' attention does not wane.

Another incredible strategy is to administer polls or surveys during your webinar. They provide an advantageous avenue for gauging audience opinions, preferences, or understanding. They've dual benefits - while they keep the audience engaged and feeling included, they also supply valuable insights to you about the attendees.

Finally, also consider incorporating quizzes, open-ended text responses or activities like brainstorming sessions. Please remember that the ultimate goal is to create a space for relevant and robust discussions, facilitating a community-like feel amongst attendees.

8.3. Leveraging Technology To Amplify Engagement

Your potential to escalate engagement in webinars is intrinsically tied with the technologies you employ to host them. The right webinar platform can empower you to foster engagement seamlessly. Utilizing features like live chat, breakout rooms, whiteboards, screen sharing, etc., you can promote interaction amongst attendees and build an enriched experience.

A strategically placed Call-to-Action (CTA) during the webinar can also motivate attendees to take the desired action quickly. It might include subscribing to a newsletter, purchasing a product, or scheduling a demo.

Moreover, technologies also allow you to integrate gamification elements into your webinar. They enrich attendee experience and increase engagement remarkably. Leaderboards, badges, or rewards for active participation can inspire attendees to engage more.

8.4. Detailed Post-Webinar Analysis

Maximizing engagement doesn't end with the conclusion of the webinar. There's a goldmine of data available for you to scrutinize through webinar analytics. This can be used to understand which parts of the webinar garnered high engagement and which ones fell flat, in turn helping in the enhancement of future webinars.

Post-webinar surveys can be executed too, to gain direct insights from the attendees about their experiences, reception of the content and suggestions for improvement. Responses to such surveys provide invaluable information that can shape the future of your webinar strategy.

As you embark on your journey towards maximizing attendee

engagement, remember that it isn't an overnight process. Continuous monitoring, reviewing and improving upon your efforts can only result in the desired increase in webinar engagement. The goal is to provide superior experiences for your attendees, allowing them to engage on their terms, and succeed in leaving a lasting impression. Implementing these strategies will ensure that your webinars are a hit, and you can exploit the potent arena of digital marketing to its full capacity.

Chapter 9. Analytics: Measuring Webinar and Social Media Success

In the world of online attendance channels, data and performance evaluation play a critical role. Every move made on social media or during webinars can result in a plethora of data that, when analysed correctly, can provide essential insights into your audience's behaviour and preferences. This wealth of information is the pillar upon which successful future strategies are built, marking the territory between 'trying' and 'knowing'. To fully appreciate the importance of analytics and learn how to successfully measure webinar and social media success, this chapter unravels in three detailed sections: Essentials of Webinar Analytics, Social Media Analytics 101, and Overcoming Challenges in Measurement and Analysis.

9.1. Essentials of Webinar Analytics

Webinars, being digital in nature, leave a trail of numerical breadcrumbs that, when picked up and analysed, have the potential to improve future webinars dramatically. When embarking on this journey, one should keep an eye out for several key performance indicators (KPIs).

The participant count is one of these vital KPIs. While it does seem quite obvious, many people underestimate its real value. It's not merely a headcount of your audience but an insight into how effectively you're driving registrations. This is equally important, both pre and post-webinar.

Another crucial KPI to monitor is the attendee engagement level. Are the attendees staying throughout the webinar or losing interest halfway? Interaction rates (questions asked, polls participated in, documents downloaded) are a goldmine of information to gauge the audience's interest. A dip in interaction might signal that the webinar content is no longer resonating with the audience.

On a closing note to this section, it's important to measure the return on investment (ROI) from your webinars. This can be evaluated based on conversion rate (number of leads converted to customers), sales generated, and the overall cost vs. benefits analysis of your webinar. These factors collectively help in measuring the financial success of your webinar.

9.2. Social Media Analytics 101

To analyze the prowess of your social media strategy, it's important to understand the end-game of your social media efforts. Is it brand awareness? Customer engagement? Lead generation? Or is it driven by sales? Once this is defined, matching KPIs can be tracked accurately.

Starting from the ground up, the first and foremost KPI to monitor is your followers count. This number can provide insights about your growing (or stagnating) influence on social media.

Engagement rate, another vital KPI, refers to how actively your audience interacts with your posts. This includes reactions, comments, shares, and link clicks. For webinars, the click-through rate (CTR) of the webinar promotion posts is paramount. The higher the CTR, the more likely your audience is interested in your webinars.

Social media sentiment analysis serves as a means to assess your brand's health. By analysing positive, negative, and neutral mentions, you can gauge your audience's overall perception and opinion about your brand and webinars.

Finally, tracking conversions would help you quantify the impact of your social media efforts on your business's bottom line. A strong social media strategy should ultimately drive traffic to your webinars, generate leads, and contribute to sales.

9.3. Overcoming Challenges in Measurement and Analysis

While webinar and social media analytics are potent tools, they come with their set of challenges. One predominant obstacle is data overload. With a vast volume of data available, it can be difficult to differentiate meaningful information from noise.

This challenge can be overcome by focusing on your primary objectives and correlating them directly to the KPIs relevant to your strategy. Using comprehensive analytics tools can also significantly ease the process by presenting data in a more digestible form.

Another significant challenge is the rapidly evolving technology and measurement metrics. As new social media platforms emerge and webinar tools advance, the analytics field is constantly changing. Staying current with these changes is vital, making continuous learning and adaptability essential.

Lastly, attributing success correctly between webinar and social media efforts could pose a challenge. For instance, a spike in webinar sign-ups could be due to a successful social media campaign, a high-quality webinar topic, or a combination of both. Utilising smart attribution models can help in accurately ascertaining the contributions of each channel.

In the rapidly expanding digital arena, the importance of data cannot be overstated. By leveraging analytics in webinars and social media, you can gain invaluable insights into your audience and their preferences. When harnessed correctly, this information can become the building blocks to a superior, more tailored online strategy, driving your business forward in the digital sphere with tremendous efficacy. So next time you embark on your digital venture, remember, the power of success lies in not just 'doing', but 'measuring' what you do.

Chapter 10. The Future of Social Media and Webinar Confluence

As we set our vision upon the fast-approaching horizon, we come to encounter a kaleidoscopic world where social media and webinars become increasingly intertwined. Be prepared to tread on this unending journey where we discuss the future complexities, opportunities, and potential challenges that await us in the evolving world of social media and webinars.

10.1. Revolution in Interactivity

A prominent shift in the confluence of social media and webinars is the increasing importance of interactivity. Interactive elements are rapidly becoming an integral part of social media strategies and webinar formats. The driving force propelling this change is the audience's heightened craving for immersive experiences and personalized journeys.

Engagement, once a buzzword, now has a profound implication when designing social media campaigns and planning webinar activities. Incorporation of Q&A sessions, live polling, and feedback surveys is becoming increasingly warranted. The concept of role-playing games, a strategy previously confined to educational structures and gaming platforms, is carving its niche in social media advertising and webinar presentations. This technique, often combined with storytelling, allows for self-guided discovery, making the experience more memorable and impacting the product's overall appeal.

10.2. The Surge of Machine Learning and AI

It's no secret that machine learning and artificial intelligence (AI) are fundamentally changing the face of digital marketing. They efficiently gather and analyze vast amounts of data at accelerated rates, which can further be leveraged for strategic purposes.

Companies embracing AI can predict consumer behavior more accurately and further enhance audience segmentation. Tailored content can then be created based on these insights, resulting in highly personalized webinar experiences or social media content that resonates with the preferences of their targeted individual viewers. AI can also automate previously manual processes such as sharing social media posts and conducting post-webinar follow-ups, allowing businesses to focus more on creative aspects like planning and content development.

10.3. Emergence of Alternate Reality Experiences

The combo of webinar and social media is already a potent platform when it comes to educating and engaging an audience. Yet, trends indicate that new technologies such as Virtual Reality (VR) and Augmented Reality (AR) will raise this bar higher, accommodating an even more immersive experience.

These technologies can transform static webinars into dynamic interactive sessions, and social media promotions into enticing, virtually tangible experiences. Imagine a webinar where participants virtually walk through an assembly line or an art gallery, fostering a deeper understanding of the topic at hand. On social media, AR filters can be utilized to showcase product features more effectively, thereby boosting promotional content.

10.4. The Importance of Data Privacy

With the explosion of data generated by digital campaigns and intricate profiling of audiences, businesses are faced with the critical responsibility of ensuring data privacy. As we move forward, stringent data protection practices will need to be built into the core of social media strategies and webinar planning.

Both social media platforms and webinar tools must keep pace with the evolving landscape of data regulations, ensuring adherence to laws such as the General Data Protection Regulation (GDPR) in Europe and the California Consumer Privacy Act (CCPA) in the United States. The audience will look favorably at businesses proactive about defending their data, and the process of audience trust building will move beyond good content to encompass robust privacy shields as well.

Each of these facets is a signpost guiding us towards the convergence of social media and webinars in the future. Organizations need to incorporate these trends into their digital strategy if they aim to sustain and thrive in an environment marked by ever-changing digital behavior and technological advancements. With success comes the reimagining of the marketing landscape through this confluence, paving the way towards a future replete with untapped potential.

Chapter 11. Case Studies: Successful Brands in Social Media and Webinar Mix

To truly paint the holistic picture of the fusion of social media and webinars, we journey into the chronicles of companies who actualised these digital marketing strategies, leading to triumphant successes. Their stories are testimony to the potency of embracing digital trends to reach target audiences, enhance engagement and amplify business growth.

11.1. Social Media & Webinar Success: The Story of Brand A

Tagged by many as a visionary in digital marketing trends, Brand A's accomplishment presents a captivating narrative. Initially, Brand A was grappling with a weakened market position due to low online engagement. Recognizing the underutilisation of its social media platforms and the lack of webinars, the company decided to marry the two strategies to not only increase engagement, but also visibility.

Firstly, Brand A leveraged the power of webinars to create valuable, informative content targeting their audience's pain points. They repurposed content from previous blog posts, eBooks, and whitepapers to deliver a cohesive narrative in their webinars. The webinars not only satisfied a thirst for knowledge amongst their audiences, but they simultaneously positioned Brand A as an industry thought leader.

Social media fell into the equation as the chosen vessel to promote these webinars. Using Facebook, LinkedIn, and Twitter, they consistently shared information about upcoming webinars. They created and shared visually appealing graphics, short video clips, and easy-to-consume infographics extracted from the webinars. Brand A also pioneered the use of paid promotion on these platforms, targeting demographics that paralleled their ideal customer profile.

The result was awe-inspiring; not only did Brand A witness an increase in webinar sign-ups, but their social media followings also surged, resulting in a strengthened market position and increased sales.

11.2. Brand B's Tactical Blend of Social Media & Webinar

Brand B distinguished itself in the industry with a unique approach towards sealing the gap in customer knowledge. The company faced the challenge of communicating complex, technical information to their clients. They found the solution in the strategic coupling of social media and webinars.

The company structured its webinars to be digestible, interactive, and fun learning experiences that broke down complex information into relatable context. The webinar content broadly covered industry trends, product tutorials, and offered a platform for Q&A sessions where participants could engage directly with Brand B's experts.

Their social media strategy was the magic wand that ensured widespread webinar visibility. Aside from routinely sharing webinar registration links, Brand B ran interactive, teaser campaigns. These campaigns would provide glimpses into the webinar's content, increasing anticipation amongst potential participants.

The approach not only expanded Brand B's customer base but also enhanced their reputation as a brand making technical knowledge accessible which ultimately led to increased loyalty, trust, and growth in revenue.

11.3. The Breakthrough Approach of Brand C

Innovation rests at the heart of Brand C's commitment to better serve their clients. As part of its strategy, Brand C adopted a groundbreaking approach to webinars – hosting co-branded webinars with established influencers in their industry. These webinars featured renowned experts to discuss industry trends and provide insights, adding credibility and pulling large audiences.

Promotion of these webinars took on a life of its own through social media. Brand C, together with the influencers, utilised their social media platforms to spread the word. They crafted compelling narratives around the influencers, the topics, and the value that attendees would gain, creating massive hype around the webinars.

This disruptive approach resulted in exponential growth in webinar attendees, widened the scope of their brand visibility to untapped markets, increased their social media engagement, and enhanced their reputation as an industry trailblazer, leading to a significant spike in their market share.

In conclusion, these case studies illustrate the potential social media and webinars, when intertwined, hold for businesses. They demonstrate how a strategically planned mix of the two can transform companies' digital landscape, boosting their online engagement, and amplifying their growth trajectory. The route they took to success is strewn with innovative uses of digital tools, with creativity and experimentation as their driving force. With the insights shared, it is now time for your brand to embark on its path, capacitated to drive higher online attendance and engagement.

www.ingramcontent.com/pod-product-compliance
Lightning Source LLC
Chambersburg PA
CBHW060857260726
48661CB00008B/3315